Fruit-(

C000128899

Copyright © 2003 BookSurge LLC
All rights reserved.

ISBN 1-59456-802-2

To order additional copies, please contact us.
BookSurge, LLC
www.booksurge.com
1-866-308-6235
orders@booksurge.com

Fruit-Gathering

Rabindranath Tagore

BookSurge Classics
Title No.802
2003

Fruit-Gathering

I

BID me and I shall gather my fruits to bring them in full baskets into your courtyard, though some are lost and some not ripe.

For the season grows heavy with its fulness, and there is a plaintive shepherd's pipe in the shade.

Bid me and I shall set sail on the river.

The March wind is fretful, fretting the languid waves into murmurs.

The garden has yielded its all, and in the weary hour of evening the call comes from your house on the shore in the sunset.

II

MY life when young was like a flower—a flower that loosens a petal or two from her abundance and never feels the loss when the spring breeze comes to beg at her door.

Now at the end of youth my life is like a fruit, having nothing to spare, and waiting to offer herself completely with her full burden of sweetness.

III

Is summer's festival only for fresh blossoms and not
　　also for withered leaves and faded flowers?
Is the song of the sea in tune only with the rising
　　waves?
Does it not also sing with the waves that fall?
Jewels are woven into the carpet where stands my king,
　　but there are patient clods waiting to be touched
　　by his feet.
Few are the wise and the great who sit by my Master,
　　but he has taken the foolish in his arms and made
　　me his servant for ever.

IV

I WOKE and found his letter with the morning.
I do not know what it says, for I cannot read.
I shall leave the wise man alone with his books, I shall
    not trouble him, for who knows if he can read what
    the letter says.
Let me hold it to my forehead and press it to my heart.
When the night grows still and stars come out one by
    one I will spread it on my lap and stay silent.
The rustling leaves will read it aloud to me, the rushing
    stream will chant it, and the seven wise stars will
    sing it to me from the sky.
I cannot find what I seek, I cannot understand what
    I would learn; but this unread letter has lightened
    my burdens and turned my thoughts into songs.

V

A HANDFUL of dust could hide your signal when I did
   not know its meaning.
Now that I am wiser I read it in all that hid it before.
It is painted in petals of flowers; waves flash it from
   their foam; hills hold it high on their summits.
I had my face turned from you, therefore I read the
   letters awry and knew not their meaning.

VI

WHERE roads are made I lose my way.

In the wide water, in the blue sky there is no line of a track.

The pathway is hidden by the birds' wings, by the star-fires, by the flowers of the wayfaring seasons.

And I ask my heart if its blood carries the wisdom of the unseen way.

VII

ALAS, I cannot stay in the house, and home has become no home to me, for the eternal *Stranger calls, he is going along the road.*

The sound of his footfall knocks at my breast; it pains me!

The wind is up, the sea is moaning. I leave all my cares and doubts to follow the homeless tide, for the Stranger calls me, he is going along the road.

VIII

BE ready to launch forth, my heart! and let those linger
    who must.
For your name has been called in the morning sky.
Wait for none!
The desire of the bud is for the night and dew, but the
    blown flower cries for the freedom of light.
Burst your sheath, my heart, and come forth!

IX

WHEN I lingered among my hoarded treasure I felt
like a worm that feeds in the dark upon the fruit
where it was born.

I leave this prison of decay.

I care not to haunt the mouldy stillness, for I go in
search of everlasting youth; I throw away all that is
not one with my life nor as light as my laughter.

I run through time and, O my heart, in your chariot
dances the poet who sings while he wanders.

X

You took my hand and drew me to your side, made me sit on the high seat before all men, till I became timid, unable to stir and walk my own way; doubting and debating at every step lest I should tread upon any thorn of their disfavour.

I am freed at last!

The blow has come, the drum of insult sounded, my seat is laid low in the dust.

My paths are open before me.

My wings are full of the desire of the sky.

I go to join the shooting stars of midnight, to plunge into the profound shadow.

I am like the storm-driven cloud of summer that, having cast off its crown of gold, hangs as a sword the thunderbolt upon a chain of lightning.

In desperate joy I run upon the dusty path of the despised; I draw near to your final welcome.

The child finds its mother when it leaves her womb.

When I am parted from you, thrown out from your household, I am free to see your face.

XI

IT decks me only to mock me, this jewelled chain of
 mine.
It bruises me when on my neck, it strangles me when I
 struggle to tear it off.
It grips my throat, it chokes my singing.
Could I but offer it to your hand, my Lord, I would be
 saved.
Take it from me, and in exchange bind me to you with a
 garland, for I am ashamed to stand before you with
 this jewelled chain on my neck.

XII

FAR below flowed the Jumna, swift and clear, above
   frowned the jutting bank.
Hills dark with the woods and scarred with the torrents
   were gathered around.
Govinda, the great Sikh teacher, sat on the rock reading
   scriptures, when Raghunath, his disciple, proud of
   his wealth, caine and bowed to him and said, "I
   have brought my poor present unworthy of your
   acceptance."
Thus saying he displayed before the teacher a pair of
   gold bangles wrought with costly stones.
The master took up one of them, twirling it round his
   finger, and the diamonds darted shafts of light.
Suddenly it slipped from his hand and rolled down the
   bank into the water.
"Alas," screamed Raghunath, and jumped into the
   stream.
The teacher set his eyes upon his book, and the water
   held and hid what it stole and went its way.
The daylight faded when Raghunath came back to the
   teacher tired and dripping.
He panted and said, "I can still get it back if you show
   me where it fell."
The teacher took up the remaining bangle and throwing
   it into the water said, "It is there."

XIII

To move is to meet you every moment,
Fellow-traveller!
It is to sing to the falling of your feet.
He whom your breath touches does not glide by the
shelter of the bank.
He spreads a reckless sail to the wind and rides the
turbulent water.
He who throws his doors open and steps onward
receives your greeting.
He does not stay to count his gain or to mourn his loss;
his heart beats the drum for his march, for that is
to march with you every step,
Fellow-traveller!

XIV

MY portion of the best in this world will come from
  your hands: such was your promise.
Therefore your light glistens in my tears.
I fear to be led by others lest I miss you waiting in some
  road corner to be my guide.
I walk my own wilful way till my very folly tempts you
  to my door.
For I have your promise that my portion of the best in
  this world will come from your hands.

XV

YOUR speech is simple, my Master, but not theirs who
    talk of you.
I understand the voice of your stars and the silence of
    your trees.
I know that my heart would open like a flower; that my
    life has filled itself at a hidden fountain.
Your songs, like birds from the lonely land of snow, are
    winging to build their nests in my heart against the
    warmth of its April, and I am content to wait for
    the merry season.

XVI

THEY knew the way and went to seek you along the
   narrow lane, but I wandered abroad into the night
   for I was ignorant.
I was not schooled enough to be afraid of you in
   the dark, therefore I came upon your doorstep
   unaware.
The wise rebuked me and bade me be gone, for I had
   not come by the lane.
I turned away in doubt, but you held me fast, and their
   scolding became louder every day.

XVII

I BROUGHT out my earthen lamp from my house and
   cried, "Come, children, I will light your path!"
The night was still dark when I returned, leaving the
   road to its silence, crying, "Light me, O Fire! for
   my earthen lamp lies broken in the dust!"

XVIII

No: it is not yours to open buds into blossoms.

Shake the bud, strike it; it is beyond your power to make it blossom.

Your touch soils it, you tear its petals to pieces and strew them in the dust.

But no colours appear, and no perfume.

Ah! it is not for you to open the bud into a blossom.

He who can open the bud does it so simply.

He gives it a glance, and the life-sap stirs through its veins.

At his breath the flower spreads its wings and flutters in the wind.

Colours flush out like heart-longings, the perfume betrays a sweet secret.

He who can open the bud does it so simply.

XIX

SUDÂS, the gardener, plucked from his tank the last
lotus left by the ravage of winter and went to sell it
to the king at the palace gate.

There he met a traveller who said to him, "Ask your
price for the last lotus, — I shall offer it to Lord
Buddha."

Sudâs said, "If you pay one golden mâshâ it will be
yours.

The traveller paid it.

At that moment the king came out and he wished to
buy the flower, for he was on his way to see Lord
Buddha, and he thought, "It would be a fine thing
to lay at his feet the lotus that bloomed in winter."

When the gardener said he had been offered a golden
mâshâ the king offered him ten, but the traveller
doubled the price.

The gardener, being greedy, imagined a greater gain
from him for whose sake they were bidding. He
bowed and said, "I cannot sell this lotus."

In the hushed shade of the mango grove beyond the
city wall Sudâs stood before Lord Buddha, on
whose lips sat the silence of love and whose eyes
beamed peace like the morning star of the dew-
washed autumn.

Sudâs looked in his face and put the lotus at his feet and
bowed his head to the dust.

Buddha smiled and asked, "What is your wish, my
    son?"

Sudâs cried, "The least touch of your feet."

XX

MAKE me thy poet, O Night, veiled Night!

There are some who have sat speechless for ages in thy shadow; let me utter their songs.

Take me up on thy chariot without wheels, running noiselessly from world to world, thou queen in the palace of time, thou darkly beautiful!

Many a questioning mind has stealthily entered thy courtyard and roamed through thy lampless house seeking for answers.

From many a heart, pierced with the arrow of joy from the hands of the Unknown, have burst forth glad chants, shaking the darkness to its foundation.

Those wakeful souls gaze in the starlight in wonder at the treasure they have suddenly found.

Make me their poet, O Night, the poet of thy fathomless silence.

XXI

I WILL meet one day the Life within me, the joy that
hides in my life, though the days perplex my path
with their idle dust.

I have known it in glimpses, and its fitful breath has
come upon me, making my thoughts fragrant for
a while.

I will meet one day the Joy without me that dwells
behind the screen of light—and will stand in the
overflowing solitude where all things are seen as by
their creator.

XXII

THIS autumn morning is tired with excess of light, and
    if your songs grow fitful and languid give me your
    flute awhile.
I shall but play with it as the whim takes me,—now take
    it on my lap, now touch it with my lips, now keep it
    by my side on the grass.
But in the solemn evening stillness I shall gather
    flowers, to deck it with wreaths, I shall fill it with
    fragrance; I shall worship it with the lighted lamp.
Then at night I shall come to you and give you back
    your flute.
You will play on it the music of midnight when the
    lonely crescent moon wanders among the stars.

XXIII

THE poet's mind floats and dances on the waves of life
    amidst the voices of wind and water.
Now when the sun has set and the darkened sky draws
    upon the sea like drooping lashes upon a weary eye
    it is time to take away his pen, and let his thoughts
    sink into the bottom of the deep amid the eternal
    secret of that silence.

XXIV

THE night is dark and your slumber is deep in the hush
   of my being.
Wake, O Pain of Love, for I know not how to open the
   door, and I stand outside.
The hours wait, the stars watch, the wind is still, the
   silence is heavy in my heart.
Wake, Love, wake! brim my empty cup, and with a
   breath of song ruffle the night.

XXV

THE bird of the morning sings.

Whence has he word of the morning before the morning breaks, and when the dragon night still holds the sky in its cold black coils?

Tell me, bird of the morning, how, through the twofold night of the sky and the leaves, he found his way into your dream, the messenger out of the east?

The world did not believe you when you cried, "The sun is on his way, the night is no more."

O sleeper, awake!

Bare your forehead, waiting for the first blessing of light, and sing with the bird of the morning in glad faith.

XXVI

THE beggar in me lifted his lean hands to the starless sky and cried into night's ear with his hungry voice.

His prayers were to the blind Darkness who lay like a fallen god in a desolate heaven of lost hopes.

The cry of desire eddied round a chasm of despair, a wailing bird circling its empty nest.

But when morning dropped anchor at the rim of the East, the beggar in me leapt and cried:

"Blessed am I that the deaf night denied me—that its coffer was empty."

He cried, "O Life, O Light, you are precious! and precious is the joy that at last has known you!"

XXVII

SANÂTAN was telling his beads by the Ganges when
a Brahmin in rags came to him and said, "Help me,
I am poor!"

"My alms-bowl is all that is my own," said Sanâtan, "I
have given away everything I had."

"But my lord Shiva came to me in my dreams," said the
Brahmin, "and counselled me to come to you."

Sanâtan suddenly remembered he had picked up a
stone without price among the pebbles on the
river-bank, and thinking that some one might need
it hid it in the sands.

He pointed out the spot to the Brahmin, who wondering
dug up the stone.

The Brahmin sat on the earth and mused alone till the
sun went down behind the trees, and cowherds
went home with their cattle.

Then he rose and came slowly to Sanâtan and said,
"Master, give me the least fraction of the wealth
that disdains all the wealth of the world."

And he threw the precious stone into the water.

XXVIII

TIME after time I came to your gate with raised hands,
     asking for more and yet more.

You gave and gave, now in slow measure, now in sudden
     excess.

I took some, and some things I let drop; some lay heavy
     on my hands; some I made into playthings and
     broke them when tired; till the wrecks and the
     hoard of your gifts grew immense, hiding you, and
     the ceaseless expectation wore my heart out.

Take, oh take — has now become my cry.

Shatter all from this beggar's bowl: put out this lamp of
     the importunate watcher: hold my hands, raise me
     from the still-gathering heap of your gifts into the
     bare infinity of your uncrowded presence.

XXIX

YOU have set me among those who are defeated.

I know it is not for me to win, nor to leave the game.

I shall plunge into the pool although but to sink to the bottom.

I shall play the game of my undoing.

I shall stake all I have and when I lose my last penny I shall stake myself, and then I think I shall have won through my utter defeat.

XXX

A SMILE of mirth spread over the sky when you dressed my heart in rags and sent her forth into the road to beg.

She went from door to door, and many a time when her bowl was nearly full she was robbed.

At the end of the weary day she came to your palace gate holding up her pitiful bowl, and you came and took her hand and seated her beside you on your throne.

XXXI

"WHO among you will take up the duty of feeding the
hungry?" Lord Buddha asked his followers when
famine raged at Shravasti.

Ratnâkar, the banker, hung his head and said, "Much
more is needed than all my wealth to feed the
hungry."

Jaysen, the chief of the King's army, said, "I would
gladly give my life's blood, but there is not enough
food in my house."

Dharmapâal, who owned broad acres of land, said with
a sigh, "The drought demon has sucked my fields
dry. I know not how to pay King's dues."

Then rose Supriyâ, the mendicant's daughter.

She bowed to all and meekly said, "I will feed the
hungry."

"How!" they cried in surprise. "How can you hope to
fulfil that vow?"

"I am the poorest of you all," said Supriyâ, "that is my
strength. I have my coffer and my store at each of
your houses."

XXXII

MY king was unknown to me, therefore when he
claimed his tribute I was bold to think I would
hide myself leaving my debts unpaid.

I fled and fled behind my day's work and my night's
dreams.

But his claims followed me at every breath I drew.

Thus I came to know that I am known to him and no
place left which is mine.

Now I wish to lay my all before his feet, and gain the
right to my place in his kingdom.

XXXIII

WHEN I thought I would mould you, an image from
my life for men to worship, I brought my dust and
desires and all my coloured delusions and dreams.
When I asked you to mould with my life an image from
your heart for you to love, you brought your fire
and force, and truth, loveliness and peace.

XXXIV

"SIRE," announced the servant to the King, "the saint
Narottam has never deigned to enter your royal
temple.

"He is singing God's praise under the trees by the open
road. The temple is empty of worshippers.

"They flock round him like bees round the white lotus,
leaving the golden jar of honey unheeded."

The King, vexed at heart, went to the spot where
Narottam sat on the grass.

He asked him, "Father, why leave my temple of the
golden dome and sit on the dust outside to preach
God's love?"

"Because God is not there in your temple," said
Narottam.

The King frowned and said, "Do you know, twenty
millions of gold went to the making of that marvel
of art, and it was consecrated to God with costly
rites?"

"Yes, I know it," answered Narottam. "It was in that
year when thousands of your people whose houses
had been burned stood vainly asking for help at
your door.

"And God said, 'The poor creature who can give no
shelter to his brothers would build my house!'

"And he took his place with the shelterless under the
trees by the road.

"And that golden bubble is empty of all but hot vapour
    of pride."

The King cried in anger, "Leave my land."

Calmly said the saint, "Yes, banish me where you have
    banished my God."

XXXV

THE trumpet lies in the dust.
The wind is weary, the light is dead.
Ah, the evil day!
Come, fighters, carrying your flags, and singers, with
　　your war-songs!
Come, pilgrims of the march, hurrying on your
　　journey!
The trumpet lies in the dust waiting for us.
I was on my way to the temple with my evening
　　offerings, seeking for a place of rest after the day's
　　dusty toil: hoping my hurts would be healed and
　　the stains in my garment washed white, when I
　　found thy trumpet lying in the dust.
Was it not the hour for me to light my evening lamp?
Had not the night sung its lullaby to the stars?
O thou blood-red rose, my poppies of sleep have paled
　　and faded!
I was certain my wanderings were over and my debts all
　　paid when suddenly I came upon thy trumpet lying
　　in the dust.
Strike my drowsy heart with thy spell of youth!
Let my joy in life blaze up in fire. Let the shafts of
　　awakening fly through the heart of night, and a
　　thrill of dread shake blindness and palsy.
I have come to raise thy trumpet from the dust.

Sleep is no more for me—my walk shall be through showers of arrows.

Some shall run out of their houses and come to my side—some shall weep.

Some in their beds shall toss and groan in dire dreams.

For to-night thy trumpet shall be sounded.

From thee I have asked peace only to find shame.

Now I stand before thee—help me to put on my armour!

Let hard blows of trouble strike fire into my life.

Let my heart beat in pain, the drum of thy victory.

My hands shall be utterly emptied to take up thy trumpet.

XXXVI

WHEN, mad in their mirth, they raised dust to soil thy
robe, O Beautiful, it made my heart sick.
I cried to thee and said, "Take thy rod of punishment
and judge them."
The morning light struck upon those eyes, red with the
revel of night; the place of the white lily greeted
their burning breath; the stars through the depth of
the sacred dark stared at their carousing—at those
that raised dust to soil thy robe, O Beautiful!
Thy judgment seat was in the flower garden, in the
birds' notes in springtime: in the shady river-
banks, where the trees muttered in answer to the
muttering of the waves.
O my Lover, they were pitiless in their passion.
They prowled in the dark to snatch thy ornaments to
deck their own desires.
When they had struck thee and thou wert pained, it
pierced me to the quick, and I cried to thee and
said, "Take thy sword, O my Lover, and judge
them!"
Ah, but thy justice was vigilant.
A mother's tears were shed on their insolence; the
imperishable faith of a lover hid their spears of
rebellion in its own wounds.
Thy judgment was in the mute pain of sleepless love:
in the blush of the chaste: in the tears of the

night of the desolate: in the pale morning-light of
forgiveness.

O Terrible, they in their reckless greed climbed thy gate
at night, breaking into thy storehouse to rob thee.

But the weight of their plunder grew immense, too
heavy to carry or to remove.

Thereupon I cried to thee and said, Forgive them, O
Terrible!

Thy forgiveness burst in storms, throwing them down,
scattering their thefts in the dust.

Thy forgiveness was in the thunder-stone; in the shower
of blood; in the angry red of the sunset.

XXXVII

UPAGUPTA, the disciple of Buddha, lay asleep on the
dust by the city wall of Mathura.

Lamps were all out, doors were all shut, and stars were
all hidden by the murky sky of August.

Whose feet were those tinkling with anklets, touching
his breast of a sudden?

He woke up startled, and the light from a woman's lamp
struck his forgiving eyes.

It was the dancing girl, starred with jewels, clouded
with a pale-blue mantle, drunk with the wine of
her youth.

She lowered her lamp and saw the young face, austerely
beautiful.

"Forgive me, young ascetic," said the woman; "graciously
come to my house. The dusty earth is not a fit bed
for you."

The ascetic answered, "Woman, go on your way; when
the time is ripe I will come to you."

Suddenly the black night showed its teeth in a flash of
lightning.

The storm growled from the corner of the sky, and the
woman trembled in fear.

. . . .

The branches of the wayside trees were aching with
blossom.

Gay notes of the flute came floating in the warm spring
air from afar.

The citizens had gone to the woods, to the festival of
flowers.

From the mid-sky gazed the full moon on the shadows
of the silent town.

The young ascetic was walking in the lonely street,
while overhead the lovesick koels urged from the
mango branches their sleepless plaint.

Upagupta passed through the city gates, and stood at
the base of the rampart.

What woman lay in the shadow of the wall at his feet,
struck with the black pestilence, her body spotted
with sores, hurriedly driven away from the town?

The ascetic sat by her side, taking her head on his knees,
and moistened her lips with water and smeared her
body with balm.

"Who are you, merciful one?" asked the woman.

"The time, at last, has come to visit you, and I am here,"
replied the young ascetic.

XXXVIII

THIS is no mere dallying of love between us, my lover.

Again and again have swooped down upon me the screaming nights of storm, blowing out my lamp: dark doubts have gathered, blotting out all stars from my sky.

Again and again the banks have burst, letting the flood sweep away my harvest, and wailing and despair have rent my sky from end to end.

This have I learnt that there are blows of pain in your love, never the cold apathy of death.

XXXIX

THE wall breaks asunder, light, like divine laughter,
     bursts in.

Victory, O Light!

The heart of the night is pierced!

With your flashing sword cut in twain the tangle of
     doubt and feeble desires!

Victory!

Come, Implacable!

Come, you who are terrible in your whiteness.

O Light, your drum sounds in the march of fire, and the
     red torch is held on high; death dies in a burst of
     splendour!

XL

O FIRE, my brother, I sing victory to you.

You are the bright red image of fearful freedom.

You swing your arms in the sky, you sweep your
    impetuous fingers across the harp-string, your
    dance music is beautiful.

When my days are ended and the gates are opened you
    will burn to ashes this cordage of hands and feet.

My body will be one with you, my heart will be caught
    in the whirls of your frenzy, and the burning heat
    that was my life will flash up and mingle itself in
    your flame.

XLI

THE Boatman is out crossing the wild sea at night.

The mast is aching because of its full sails filled with the violent wind.

Stung with the night's fang the sky falls upon the sea, poisoned with black fear.

The waves dash their heads against the dark unseen, and the Boatman is out crossing the wild sea.

The Boatman is out, I know not for what tryst, startling the night with the sudden white of his sails.

I know not at what shore, at last, he lands to reach the silent courtyard where the lamp is burning and to find her who sits in the dust and waits.

What is the quest that makes his boat care not for storm nor darkness?

Is it heavy with gems and pearls?

Ah, no, the Boatman brings with him no treasure, but only a white rose in his hand and a song on his lips.

It is for her who watches alone at night with her lamp burning.

She dwells in the wayside hut. Her loose hair flies in the wind and hides her eyes.

The storm shrieks through her broken doors, the light flickers in her earthen lamp flinging shadows on the walls.

Through the howl of the winds she hears him call her
name, she whose name is unknown.

It is long since the Boatman sailed. It will be long before
the day breaks and he knocks at the door.

The drums will not be beaten and none will know.

Only light shall fill the house, blessed shall be the dust,
and the heart glad.

All doubts shall vanish in silence when the Boatman
comes to the shore.

XLII

I CLING to this living raft, my body, in the narrow
    stream of my earthly years.
I leave it when the crossing is over. And then?
I do not know if the light there and the darkness are
    the same.
The Unknown is the perpetual freedom:
He is pitiless in his love.
He crushes the shell for the pearl, dumb in the prison
    of the dark.
You muse and weep for the days that are done, poor
    heart!
Be glad that days are to come!
The hour strikes, O pilgrim!
It is time for you to take the parting of the ways!
His face will be unveiled once again and you shall
    meet.

XLIII

OVER the relic of Lord Buddha King Bimbisâr built a shrine, a salutation in white marble.

There in the evening would come all the brides and daughters of the King's house to offer flowers and light lamps.

When the son became king in his time he washed his father's creed away with blood, and lit sacrificial fires with its sacred books.

The autumn day was dying. The evening hour of worship was near.

Shrimati, the queen's maid, devoted to Lord Buddha, having bathed in holy water, and decked the golden tray with lamps and fresh white blossoms, silently raised her dark eyes to the queen's face.

The queen shuddered in fear and said, "Do you not know, foolish girl, that death is the penalty for whoever brings worship to Buddha's shrine?

"Such is the king's will."

Shrimati bowed to the queen, and turning away from her door came and stood before Amitâ, the newly wed bride of the king's son.

A mirror of burnished gold on her lap, the newly wed bride was braiding her dark long tresses and painting the red spot of good luck at the parting of her hair.

Her hands trembled when she saw the young maid, and

she cried, "What fearful peril would you bring me!
Leave me this instant."

Princess Shuklâ sat at the window reading her book of
romance by the light of the setting sun.

She started when she saw at her door the maid with the
sacred offerings.

Her book fell down from her lap, and she whispered
in Shrimati's ears, "Rush not to death, daring
woman!"

Shrimati walked from door to door. She raised her head
and cried, "O women of the king's house, hasten!

"The time for our Lord's worship is come!"

Some shut their doors in her face and some reviled her.

The last gleam of daylight faded from the bronze dome
of the palace tower.

Deep shadows settled in street corners: the bustle of
the city was hushed: the gong at the temple of
Shiva announced the time of the evening prayer.

In the dark of the autumn evening, deep as a limpid
lake, stars throbbed with light, when the guards
of the palace garden were startled to see through
the trees a row of lamps burning at the shrine of
Buddha.

They ran with their swords unsheathed, crying, "Who
are you, foolish one, reckless of death?"

"I am Shrimati," replied a sweet voice, "the servant of
Lord Buddha."

The next moment her heart's blood coloured the cold
marble with its red.

And in the still hour of stars died the light of the last
lamp of worship at the foot of the shrine.

XLIV

THE day that stands between you and me makes her last bow of farewell.

The night draws her veil over her face, and hides the one lamp burning in my chamber.

Your dark servant comes noiselessly and spreads the bridal carpet for you to take your seat there alone with me in the wordless silence till night is done.

XLV

MY night has passed on the bed of sorrow, and my eyes
are tired. My heavy heart is not yet ready to meet
morning with its crowded joys.
Draw a veil over this naked light, beckon aside from me
this glaring flash and dance of life.
Let the mantle of tender darkness cover me in its folds,
and cover my pain awhile from the pressure of the
world.

XLVI

THE time is past when I could repay her for all that I received.

Her night has found its morning and thou hast taken her to thy arms: and to thee I bring my gratitude and my gifts that were for her.

For all hurts and offences to her I come to thee for forgiveness.

I offer to thy service those flowers of my love that remained in bud when she waited for them to open.

XLVII

I FOUND a few old letters of mine carefully hidden in
   her box—a few small toys for her memory to play
   with.

With a timorous heart she tried to steal these trifles
   from time's turbulent stream, and said, "These are
   mine only!"

Ah, there is no one now to claim them, who can pay
   their price with loving care, yet here they are still.

Surely there is love in this world to save her from utter
   loss, even like this love of hers that saved these
   letters with such fond care.

XLVIII

BRING beauty and order into my forlorn life, woman,
as you brought them into my house when you
lived.

Sweep away the dusty fragments of the hours, fill the
empty jars, and mend all that has been neglected.

Then open the inner door of the shrine, light the candle,
and let us meet there in silence before our God.

XLIX

THE pain was great when the strings were being tuned,
   my Master!
Begin your music, and let me forget the pain; let me feel
   in beauty what you had in your mind through those
   pitiless days.
The waning night lingers at my doors, let her take her
   leave in songs.
Pour your heart into my life strings, my Master, in tunes
   that descend from your stars.

L

IN the lightning flash of a moment I have seen the
  immensity of your creation in my life—creation
  through many a death from world to world.
I weep at my unworthiness when I see my life in the
  hands of the unmeaning hours,—but when I see
  it in your hands I know it is too precious to be
  squandered among shadows.

LI

I KNOW that at the dim end of some day the sun will
bid me its farewell.

Shepherds will play their pipes beneath the banyan
trees, and cattle graze on the slope by the river,
while my days will pass into the dark.

This is my prayer, that I may know before I leave why
the earth called me to her arms.

Why her night's silence spoke to me of stars, and her
daylight kissed my thoughts into flower.

Before I go may I linger over my last refrain, completing
its music, may the lamp be lit to see your face and
the wreath woven to crown you.

LII

WHAT music is that in whose measure the world is
rocked?

We laugh when it beats upon the crest of life, we shrink
in terror when it returns into the dark.

But the play is the same that comes and goes with the
rhythm of the endless music.

You hide your treasure in the palm of your hand, and we
cry that we are robbed.

But open and shut your palm as you will, the gain and
the loss are the same.

At the game you play with your own self you lose and
win at once.

LIII

I HAVE kissed this world with my eyes and my limbs; I have wrapt it within my heart in numberless folds; I have flooded its days and nights with thoughts till the world and my life have grown one,—and I love my life because I love the light of the sky so enwoven with me.

If to leave this world be as real as to love it—then there must be a meaning in the meeting and the parting of life.

If that love were deceived in death, then the canker of this deceit would eat into all things, and the stars would shrivel and grow black.

LIV

THE Cloud said to me, "I vanish"; the Night said, "I plunge into the fiery dawn."

The Pain said, "I remain in deep silence as his footprint."

"I die into the fulness," said my life to me.

The Earth said, "My lights kiss your thoughts every moment."

"The days pass," Love said, "but I wait for you."

Death said, "I ply the boat of your life across the sea."

LV

TULSIDAS, the poet, was wandering, deep in thought, by the Ganges, in that lonely spot where they burn their dead.

He found a woman sitting at the feet of the corpse of her dead husband, gaily dressed as for a wedding.

She rose as she saw him, bowed to him, and said, "Permit me, Master, with your blessing, to follow my husband to heaven."

"Why such hurry, my daughter?" asked Tulsidas. "Is not this earth also His who made heaven?"

"For heaven I do not long," said the woman. "I want my husband."

Tulsidas smiled and said to her, "Go back to your home, my child. Before the month is over you will find your husband."

The woman went back with glad hope. Tulsidas came to her every day and gave her high thoughts to think, till her heart was filled to the brim with divine love.

When the month was scarcely over, her neighbours came to her, asking, "Woman, have you found your husband?"

The widow smiled and said, "I have."

Eagerly they asked, "Where is he?"

"In my heart is my lord, one with me," said the woman.

LVI

You came for a moment to my side and touched me
with the great mystery of the woman that there is
in the heart of creation.

She who is ever returning to God his own outflowing of
sweetness; she is the ever fresh beauty and youth
in nature; she dances in the bubbling streams and
sings in the morning light; she with heaving waves
suckles the thirsty earth; in her the Eternal One
breaks in two in a joy that no longer may contain
itself, and overflows in the pain of love.

LVII

WHO is she who dwells in my heart, the woman
  forlorn for ever?
I wooed her and I failed to win her. I decked her with
  wreaths and sang in her praise.
A smile shone in her face for a moment, then it faded.
"I have no joy in thee," she cried, the woman in sorrow.
I bought her jewelled anklets and fanned her with a fan
  gem-studded; I made her a bed on a bedstead of
  gold.
There flickered a gleam of gladness in her eyes, then it
  died.
"I have no joy in these," she cried, the woman in
  sorrow.
I seated her upon a car of triumph and drove her from
  end to end of the earth.
Conquered hearts bowed down at her feet, and shouts
  of applause rang in the sky.
Pride shone in her eyes for a moment, then it was
  dimmed in tears.
"I have no joy in conquest," she cried, the woman in
  sorrow.
I asked her, "Tell me whom do you seek?"
She only said, "I wait for him of the unknown name."
Days pass by and she cries, "When will my beloved
  come whom I know not, and be known to me for
  ever?"

LVIII

YOURS is the light that breaks forth from the dark,
 and the good that sprouts from the cleft heart of
 strife.

Yours is the house that opens upon the world, and the
 love that calls to the battlefield.

Yours is the gift that still is a gain when everything is a
 loss, and the life that flows through the caverns of
 death.

Yours is the heaven that lies in the common dust, and
 you are there for me, you are there for all.

LIX

WHEN the weariness of the road is upon me, and the thirst of the sultry day; when the ghostly hours of the dusk throw their shadows across my life, then I cry not for your voice only, my friend, but for your touch.

There is an anguish in my heart for the burden of its riches not given to you.

Put out your hand through the night, let me hold it and fill it and keep it; let me feel its touch along the lengthening stretch of my loneliness.

LX

THE odour cries in the bud, "Ah me, the day departs, the happy day of spring, and I am a prisoner in petals!"

Do not lose heart, timid thing! Your bonds will burst, the bud will open into flower, and when you die in the fulness of life, even then the spring will live on.

The odour pants and flutters within the bud, crying, "Ah me, the hours pass by, yet I do not know where I go, or what it is I seek!"

Do not lose heart, timid thing! The spring breeze has overheard your desire, the day will not end before you have fulfilled your being.

Dark is the future to her, and the odour cries in despair, "Ah me, through whose fault is my life so unmeaning?

"Who can tell me, why I am at all?" Do not lose heart, timid thing! The perfect dawn is near when you will mingle your life with all life and know at last your purpose.

LXI

SHE is still a child, my lord.

She runs about your palace and plays, and tries to make of you a plaything as well.

She heeds not when her hair tumbles down and her careless garment drags in the dust.

She falls asleep when you speak to her and answers not—and the flower you give her in the morning slips to the dust from her hands.

When the storm bursts and darkness is over the sky she is sleepless; her dolls lie scattered on the earth and she clings to you in terror.

She is afraid that she may fail in service to you.

But with a smile you watch her at her game.

You know her.

The child sitting in the dust is your destined bride; her play will be stilled and deepened into love.

LXII

"WHAT is there but the sky, O Sun, that can hold thine
    image?"
"I dream of thee, but to serve thee I can never hope,"
    the dewdrop wept and said, "I am too small to take
    thee unto me, great lord, and my life is all tears."
"I illumine the limitless sky, yet I can yield myself up
    to a tiny drop of dew," thus the Sun said; "I shall
    become but a sparkle of light and fill you, and your
    little life will be a laughing orb."

LXIII

NOT for me is the love that knows no restraint, but like the foaming wine that having burst its vessel in a moment would run to waste.

Send me the love which is cool and pure like your rain that blesses the thirsty earth and fills the homely earthen jars.

Send me the love that would soak down into the centre of being, and from there would spread like the unseen sap through the branching tree of life, giving birth to fruits and flowers.

Send me the love that keeps the heart still with the fulness of peace.

LXIV

THE sun had set on the western margin of the river among the tangle of the forest.

The hermit boys had brought the cattle home, and sat round the fire to listen to the master, Guatama, when a strange boy came, and greeted him with fruits and flowers, and, bowing low at his feet, spoke in a bird-like voice—"Lord, I have come to thee to be taken into the path of the supreme Truth.

"My name is Satyakâma."

"Blessings be on thy head," said the master.

"Of what clan art thou, my child? It is only fitting for a Brahmin to aspire to the highest wisdom."

"Master," answered the boy, "I know not of what clan I am. I shall go and ask my mother."

Thus saying, Satyakma took leave, and wading across the shallow stream, came back to his mother's hut, which stood at the end of the sandy waste at the edge of the sleeping village.

The lamp burnt dimly in the room, and the mother stood at the door in the dark waiting for her son's return.

She clasped him to her bosom, kissed him on his hair, and asked him of his errand to the master.

"What is the name of my father, dear mother?" asked the boy.

"It is only fitting for a Brahmin to aspire to the highest wisdom, said Lord Guatama to me."

The woman lowered her eyes, and spoke in a whisper.

"In my youth I was poor and had many masters. Thou didst come to thy mother Jabâlâ's arms, my darling, who had no husband."

The early rays of the sun glistened on the tree-tops of the forest hermitage.

The students, with their tangled hair still wet with their morning bath, sat under the ancient tree, before the master.

There came Satyakâma.

He bowed low at the feet of the sage, and stood silent.

"Tell me," the great teacher asked him, "of what clan art thou?"

"My lord," he answered, "I know it not. My mother said when I asked her, 'I had served many masters in my youth, and thou hadst come to thy mother Jabâlâ's arms, who had no husband.'"

There rose a murmur like the angry hum of bees disturbed in their hive; and the students muttered at the shameless insolence of that outcast.

Master Guatama rose from his seat, stretched out his arms, took the boy to his bosom, and said, "Best of all Brahmins art thou, my child. Thou hast the noblest heritage of truth."

LXV

MAY be there is one house in this city where the gate opens for ever this morning at the touch of the sunrise, where the errand of the light is fulfilled.

The flowers have opened in hedges and gardens, and may be there is one heart that has found in them this morning the gift that has been on its voyage from endless time.

LXVI

LISTEN, my heart, in his flute is the music of the
smell of wild flowers, of the glistening leaves and
gleaming water, of shadows resonant with bees'
wings.
The flute steals his smile from my friend's lips and
spreads it over my life.

LXVII

You always stand alone beyond the stream of my songs.
The waves of my tunes wash your feet but I know not
     how to reach them.
This play of mine with you is a play from afar.
It is the pain of separation that melts into melody
     through my flute.
I wait for the time when your boat crosses over to my
     shore and you take my flute into your own hands.

LXVIII

SUDDENLY the window of my heart flew open this
morning, the window that looks out on your
heart.

I wondered to see that the name by which you know
me is written in April leaves and flowers, and I sat
silent.

The curtain was blown away for a moment between my
songs and yours.

I found that your morning light was full of my own
mute songs unsung; I thought that I would learn
them at your feet—and I sat silent.

LXIX

You were in the centre of my heart, therefore when
my heart wandered she never found you; you hid
yourself from my loves and hopes till the last, for
you were always in them.

You were the inmost joy in the play of my youth, and
when I was too busy with the play the joy was
passed by.

You sang to me in the ecstasies of my life and I forgot
to sing to you.

LXX

WHEN you hold your lamp in the sky it throws its light
on my face and its shadow falls over you.

When I hold the lamp of love in my heart its light
falls on you and I am left standing behind in the
shadow.

LXXI

O THE waves, the sky-devouring waves, glistening with light, dancing with life, the waves of eddying joy, rushing for ever.

The stars rock upon them, thoughts of every tint are cast up out of the deep and scattered on the beach of life.

Birth and death rise and fall with their rhythm, and the sea-gull of my heart spreads its wings crying in delight.

LXXII

THE joy ran from all the world to build my body.

The lights of the skies kissed and kissed her till she woke.

Flowers of hurrying summers sighed in her breath and voices of winds and water sang in her movements.

The passion of the tide of colours in clouds and in forests flowed into her life, and the music of all things caressed her limbs into shape.

She is my bride,—she has lighted her lamp in my house.

LXXIII

THE spring with its leaves and flowers has come into
    my body.
The bees hum there the morning long, and the winds
    idly play with the shadows.
A sweet fountain springs up from the heart of my
    heart.
My eyes are washed with delight like the dew-bathed
    morning, and life is quivering in all my limbs like
    the sounding strings of the lute.
Are you wandering alone by the shore of my life, where
    the tide is in flood, O lover of my endless days?
Are my dreams flitting round you like the moths with
    their many-coloured wings?
And are those your songs that are echoing in the dark
    eaves of my being?
Who but you can hear the hum of the crowded hours
    that sounds in my veins to-day, the glad steps that
    dance in my breast, the clamour of the restless life
    beating its wings in my body?

LXXIV

MY bonds are cut, my debts are paid, my door has been
opened, I go everywhere.
They crouch in their corner and weave their web of
pale hours, they count their coins sitting in the
dust and call me back.
But my sword is forged, my armour is put on, my horse
is eager to run.
I shall win my kingdom.

LXXV

IT was only the other day that I came to your earth,
    naked and nameless, with a wailing cry.

To-day my voice is glad, while you, my lord, stand aside
    to make room that I may fill my life.

Even when I bring you my songs for an offering I have
    the secret hope that men will come and love me
    for them.

You love to discover that I love this world where you
    have brought me.

LXXVI

TIMIDLY I cowered in the shadow of safety, but now, when the surge of joy carries my heart upon its crest, my heart clings to the cruel rock of its trouble.

I sat alone in a corner of my house thinking it too narrow for any guest, but now when its door is flung open by an unbidden joy I find there is room for thee and for all the world.

I walked upon tiptoe, careful of my person, perfumed, and adorned—but now when a glad whirlwind has overthrown me in the dust I laugh and roll on the earth at thy feet like a child.

LXXVII

THE world is yours at once and for ever.

And because you have no want, my king, you have no pleasure in your wealth.

It is as though it were naught. Therefore through slow time you give me what is yours, and ceaselessly win your kingdom in me.

Day after day you buy your sunrise from my heart, and you find your love carven into the image of my life.

LXXVIII

TO the birds you gave songs, the birds gave you songs
in return.

You gave me only voice, yet asked for more, and I sing.

You made your winds light and they are fleet in their
service. You burdened my hands that I myself
may lighten them, and at last, gain unburdened
freedom for your service.

You created your Earth filling its shadows with
fragments of light.

There you paused; you left me empty-handed in the
dust to create your heaven.

To all things else you give; from me you ask.

The harvest of my life ripens in the sun and the shower
till I reap more than you sowed, gladdening your
heart, O Master of the golden granary.

LXXIX

LET me not pray to be sheltered from dangers but to be
fearless in facing them.

Let me not beg for the stilling of my pain but for the
heart to conquer it.

Let me not look for allies in life's battlefield but to my
own strength.

Let me not crave in anxious fear to be saved but hope
for the patience to win my freedom.

Grant me that I may not be a coward, feeling your
mercy in my success alone; but let me find the
grasp of your hand in my failure.

LXXX

YOU did not know yourself when you dwelt alone, and
there was no crying of an errand when the wind ran
from the hither to the farther shore.

I came and you woke, and the skies blossomed with
lights.

You made me open in many flowers; rocked me in the
cradles of many forms; hid me in death and found
me again in life.

I came and your heart heaved; pain came to you and
joy.

You touched me and tingled into love.

But in my eyes there is a film of shame and in my breast
a flicker of fear; my face is veiled and I weep when
I cannot see you.

Yet I know the endless thirst in your heart for sight of
me, the thirst that cries at my door in the repeated
knockings of sunrise.

LXXXI

YOU, in your timeless watch, listen to my approaching
steps while your gladness gathers in the morning
twilight and breaks in the burst of light.

The nearer I draw to you the deeper grows the fervour
in the dance of the sea.

Your world is a branching spray of light filling your
hands, but your heaven is in my secret heart; it
slowly opens its buds in shy love.

LXXXII

I WILL utter your name, sitting alone among the shadows of my silent thoughts.

I will utter it without words, I will utter it without purpose.

For I am like a child that calls its mother an hundred times, glad that it can say "Mother."

LXXXIII

I

I FEEL that all the stars shine in me. The world breaks into my life like a flood.

The flowers blossom in my body. All the youthfulness of land and water smokes like an incense in my heart; and the breath of all things plays on my thoughts as on a flute.

II

When the world sleeps I come to your door.

The stars are silent, and I am afraid to sing.

I wait and watch, till your shadow passes by the balcony of night and I return with a full heart.

Then in the morning I sing by the roadside;

The flowers in the hedge give me answer and the morning air listens,

The travellers suddenly stop and look in my face, thinking I have called them by their names.

III

Keep me at your door ever attending to your wishes, and let me go about in your Kingdom accepting your call.

Let me not sink and disappear in the depth of languor.

Let not my life be worn out to tatters by penury of waste.

Let not those doubts encompass me,—the dust of
   distractions.

Let me not pursue many paths to gather many things.

Let me not bend my heart to the yoke of the many.

Let me hold my head high in the courage and pride of
   being your servant.

LXXXIV.

THE OARSMEN

Do you hear the tumult of death afar,
The call midst the fire-floods and poisonous clouds
—The Captain's call to the steersman to turn the ship to
    an unnamed shore,
For that time is over—the stagnant time in the port—
Where the same old merchandise is bought and sold in
    an endless round,
Where dead things drift in the exhaustion and
    emptiness of truth.
They wake up in sudden fear and ask,
"Comrades, what hour has struck?
When shall the dawn begin?"
The clouds have blotted away the stars—
Who is there then can see the beckoning finger of the
    day?
They run out with oars in hand, the beds are emptied,
    the mother prays, the wife watches by the door;
There is a wail of parting that rises to the sky,
And there is the Captain's voice in the dark:
"Come, sailors, for the time in the harbour is over!"
All the black evils in the world have overflowed their
    banks,
Yet, oarsmen, take your places with the blessing of
    sorrow in your souls!

Whom do you blame, brothers? Bow your heads down!
The sin has been yours and ours.
The heat growing in the heart of God for ages—
The cowardice of the weak, the arrogance of the strong,
     the greed of fat prosperity, the rancour of the
     wronged, pride of race, and insult to man—
Has burst God's peace, raging in storm.
Like a ripe pod, let the tempest break its heart into
     pieces, scattering thunders.
Stop your bluster of dispraise and of self-praise,
And with the calm of silent prayer on your foreheads
     sail to that unnamed shore.
We have known sins and evils every day and death we
     have known;
They pass over our world like clouds mocking us with
     their transient lightning laughter.
Suddenly they have stopped, become a prodigy,
And men must stand before them saying:
"We do not fear you, O Monster! for we have lived every
     day by conquering you,
"And we die with the faith that Peace is true, and Good
     is true, and true is the eternal One!"
If the Deathless dwell not in the heart of death,
If glad wisdom bloom not bursting the sheath of
     sorrow,
If sin do not die of its own revealment,
If pride break not under its load of decorations,
Then whence comes the hope that drives these men
     from their homes like stars rushing to their death
     in the morning light?
Shall the value of the martyrs' blood and mothers' tears

be utterly lost in the dust of the earth, not buying
Heaven with their price?

And when Man bursts his mortal bounds, is not the
Boundless revealed that moment?

LXXXV.

THE SONG OF THE DEFEATED

MY Master has bid me while I stand at the roadside, to sing the song of Defeat, for that is the bride whom He woos in secret.

She has put on the dark veil, hiding her face from the crowd, but the jewel glows on her breast in the dark.

She is forsaken of the day, and God's night is waiting for her with its lamps lighted and flowers wet with dew.

She is silent with her eyes downcast; she has left her home behind her, from her home has come that wailing in the wind.

But the stars are singing the love-song of the eternal to a face sweet with shame and suffering.

The door has been opened in the lonely chamber, the call has sounded, and the heart of the darkness throbs with awe because of the coming tryst.

LXXXVI.

THANKSGIVING

THOSE who walk on the path of pride crushing the lowly life under their tread, covering the tender green of the earth with their footprints in blood;

Let them rejoice, and thank thee, Lord, for the day is theirs.

But I am thankful that my lot lies with the humble who suffer and bear the burden of power, and hide their faces and stifle their sobs in the dark.

For every throb of their pain has pulsed in the secret depth of thy night, and every insult has been gathered into thy great silence. And the morrow is theirs.

O Sun, rise upon the bleeding hearts blossoming in flowers of the morning, and the torchlight revelry of pride shrunken to ashes.

THE END

ABOUT GREATUNPUBLISHED.COM

www.greatunpublished.com is a website that exists to serve writers and readers, and to remove some of the commercial barriers between them. When you purchase a GreatUNpublished title, whether you order it in electronic form or in a paperback volume, the author is receiving a majority of the post-production revenue.

A GreatUNpublished book is never out of stock, and always available, because each book is printed on-demand, as it is ordered.

A portion of the site's share of profits is channeled into literacy programs.

So by purchasing this title from GreatUNpublished, you are helping to revolutionize the publishing industry for the benefit of writers and readers.

And for this we thank you.